Discovering the Untouched Gems

A Comprehensive Travel Guide to Guinea Bissau"Unveiling the Vibrant Culture, Pristine Nature, and Authentic Adventures of West Africa's Hidden Paradise

Edith M.scott

Table of contents

INTRODUCTION
   a. Culture and History
Planning Your Trip
   a. Visa and Travel Document Requirements
How To Get To Guinea-Bissau
   a. Airlines and Airports
A Tour Of Bissau
   a. Options for Accommodation
   b. Food and Dining
Cities And Regions To Visit
   a. Bolama
   b.Cacheu
Natural Attractions
   a. Archipelago of Bijagos
   b.National Park of the Orango Islands
   Additional Natural Wonders
Cultural Experience
   a.Customary Holidays and Events
   c. Historical Sites and Museums
Outdoor Activities

a.Wildlife and bird watching

c.Beaches and Water Activities

Practical Travel Advice

b Transportation Safety Advice

d.Important Items to Pack

Guinea-Bissau has a tropical environment, thus it is advised to wear light, breathable clothing. Bring clothing that will shield you from the sun and insect stings.

Language and Useful Phrase

Foundational Expressions and Phrases

Safety And Health

a.Immunizations and medical preparation

b. Travel protection

Sustainable Travel and Responsible Tourism

a. Environmental and Cultural Considerations

INTRODUCTION

Guinea-Bissau is a tiny nation in West Africa that borders the Atlantic Ocean. Its official name is the Republic of Guinea-Bissau. Its northern border with Senegal and its southern and eastern borders with Guinea are shared. The Balanta, Fula, and Mandinka populations, which are the most numerous ethnic groupings in the nation, are among its diversified population. Guinea-Bissau's capital and largest city is Bissau.

Travelers can enjoy a distinctive experience in Guinea-Bissau thanks to its diverse cultural heritage. The nation is renowned for having a thriving music scene, with traditional West African rhythms, Afro-Cuban music, and Gumbe music all over the place. Additionally, the inviting aspect of the Bissau-Guinean people is a result of their warmth and friendliness.

Geography and climate

- Geographically, Guinea-Bissau has a diversified landscape. The nation is home to mangrove swamps, the Bijagós Archipelago, a UNESCO Biosphere Reserve noted for its biodiversity, and coastal plains along the

Atlantic Ocean. The Fouta Djallon plateau extends into northeastern Guinea-Bissau, where the landscape becomes hillier and more forested.

Guinea-Bissau has a tropical climate with distinct rainy and dry seasons. From June to October, the nation has a rainy season characterized by sweltering temperatures and copious amounts of precipitation. The dry season, which lasts from November to May, delivers reduced humidity and milder temperatures. While the core parts face more harsh temperatures, the coastline regions benefit from oceanic impacts.

a. Culture and History

- The history of Guinea-Bissau is extensive, having been affected by numerous empires, colonization, and independence movements. Several strong West African nations, notably the Mali Empire and the Kingdom of Gabu, were based in the area. Portuguese colonization of the region lasted for several centuries after their arrival in the 15th century and the establishment of a sizable presence.

Guinea-Bissau fought against Portuguese authority in the middle of the 20th century, and it finally declared independence in 1973. National hero Amilcar Cabral was instrumental in directing the freedom effort. His legacy is now honored all around the nation.

Guinea-Bissau has a rich cultural legacy that is influenced by many different ethnic groups. The gumbe rhythm is an essential component of the national character of Bissau-Guinea, as are traditional music and dance. The nation also has a thriving handicraft industry that creates beautiful pottery, woven linens, and delicate wood carvings.

b. Useful Information

- There are many practical things to keep in mind when organizing a vacation to Guinea-Bissau. Although Crioulo, a Creole with Portuguese roots, is widely spoken,

Portuguese is the official language. Cash is the predominant form of payment in this area, and the official currency is the West African CFA franc (XOF).

Before traveling to Guinea-Bissau, it's crucial to confirm the visa requirements and make sure you have the required documentation. For the most recent information, it is advised to contact the Bissau-Guinean embassy or consulate closest to you.

- Safety and health are also crucial factors. Before traveling to Guinea-Bissau, it is best to speak with a healthcare provider or travel clinic about any necessary vaccinations. Due to the high prevalence of malaria in the nation, it is essential to take the appropriate precautions, including applying insect repellent and sleeping under a bed net.

Osvaldo Vieira International Airport, which serves as the primary entrance point for travelers, is the international airport in Bissau. There are many ways to go about the nation, including taxis, shared vans, and mini-bus. It's crucial to exercise caution and adhere to safety precautions when taking public transit.

For a seamless and courteous trip in Guinea-Bissau, it is imperative to comprehend the regional customs and manners. A handshake and courteous talk are customary greetings that are significant. It is preferable to make a gesture with an open hand because it is considered disrespectful to the point with your finger.

Visitors may make the most of their trip to Guinea-Bissau and have a productive and happy experience by being prepared with useful information and respecting the local culture.

Planning Your Trip

2.1 Visa and Travel Document Requirements

2.2 Safety and Health

2.3 Exchange Rates and Money

2.4 Communication and Language

a. Visa and Travel Document Requirements

Make sure you have the required travel documentation before departing for Guinea-Bissau. A passport must be valid for at least six months after the desired departure date for the majority of travelers. To find out if you need a visa for entry, contact the Bissau-Guinean embassy or consulate nearest to you. Depending on your nationality and the reason for your visit, different visas may be needed. To prevent any last-minute issues, it is essential to submit your visa application well in advance.

b. Safety and Health

- Because Guinea-Bissau is in a tropical area, you should take a few health precautions before traveling there. To get the most recent information on required vaccinations, speak with a medical expert or travel clinic. Hepatitis A and B, typhoid, yellow fever, and meningococcal meningitis are among the immunizations frequently administered in Guinea-Bissau.

Given the prevalence of malaria in the nation, it is imperative to practice prevention. To avoid getting bitten by mosquitoes, seek medical advice regarding the best antimalarial treatment, and make sure you have bed nets, long-sleeved clothing, and mosquito repellent on hand.

To prevent foodborne infections, it is advised to consume bottled water and stay away from eating raw or undercooked food. Carry a small first aid kit that includes all the necessary supplies, including bandages, antiseptic cream, and any personal drugs you might need.

Being cautious and paying attention to your surroundings is essential for your safety. Keep expensive stuff hidden and watch out for pickpockets in busy places. Use safe transportation wherever possible, and stay off the streets at night, especially in remote locations.

c. Exchange Rates and Money

- The West African CFA franc (XOF) is the official unit of exchange in Guinea-Bissau. It is advised to convert money when you arrive at the airport or in a big city like Bissau. Because international credit and debit cards are not commonly used, it is advised to bring enough cash for your needs.

Banks and certain hotels provide currency exchange services. It's a good idea to carry small denominations because it could be more difficult to break larger ones. Plan your trip appropriately, as cash may be the sole accepted mode of payment outside of big cities.

Communication and Language

- Because of its colonial background, Guinea-Bissau has Portuguese as its official language. However, Crioulo, a Creole language with a Portuguese foundation, is extensively used and acts as the common language. Since English is not widely used, it can be useful to learn a few fundamental phrases in Crioulo or to keep a translation tool or phrasebook close at hand.

Although it is expanding, Guinea-Bissau's communication infrastructure can still be patchy in some places, particularly outside of big towns. Urban places have mobile phone coverage, however isolated areas may only have patchy or no coverage at all. Internet connection is provided in some hotels, cafes, and internet hubs in large cities, and local SIM cards can be acquired for mobile phone use.

A smooth and pleasurable journey to Guinea-Bissau can be made possible by being ready with the required travel documents, being aware of health and safety measures, handling currency and exchange, and becoming comfortable with the local language and communication environment.

How To Get To Guinea-Bissau

a. Airlines and Airports

Osvaldo Vieira International Airport (OXB), which is situated in Bissau, the nation's capital, is the country's primary international entry point. Regular flights are provided by some carriers, including TAP Air Portugal, Royal Air Maroc, Air Senegal, and Binter Canarias, to and from Bissau. There are connecting flights from significant international airports to Bissau.

To get the best deals and guarantee availability, it's a good idea to book your flights long in advance, especially during periods of high travel demand.

Before entering the nation, immigration and customs formalities must be finished at Osvaldo Vieira International Airport.

b. **Borders, Land, and Sea**

- Senegal and Guinea border Guinea-Bissau on land in the north, south, and east, respectively. Road and rail connections can be used to cross land borders. In the north and east, respectively, So Domingos and Caió, are the primary border crossings. Before attempting to cross a land border, it is crucial to confirm visa requirements and border policies as entry criteria can change.

Although there are few ferry services linking the Bijagós Archipelago to the mainland, there is some sea transport to Guinea-Bissau. If you intend to travel by water, it is essential to check with local authorities or travel agents for the most up-to-date information because these services are erratic and prone to change.

c. Countrywide Transportation

In Guinea-Bissau, transportation can be difficult because of the country's poor infrastructure and inconsistent road conditions. Taxis, mini-bus (also known as "toca-tocas"), and shared vans are the most popular ways to go across the nation.

- Taxis are widely accessible in cities like Bissau. As taxis frequently lack meters, it is advised to haggle the fare before setting off on the trip. Additionally practical for quick city journeys are taxis.

For lengthier domestic trips, minibus, or "toca-tocas," are a common mode of transportation. These mini buses go along predetermined routes picking up and dropping off people. When using this mode of transportation, flexibility is required because it can be busy and they might not follow precise schedules.

- The term "candongueiro," or shared vans, is another alternative for intercity transport. These vans run along predetermined routes and might be an affordable mode of transportation. However, they might not have enough room for luggage and can be cramped.

It's crucial to remember that infrastructure and road conditions in Guinea-Bissau might vary, especially in rural areas. It is best to travel during the day and to drive or take public transportation with caution. Traveling more safely and conveniently can be made easier by hiring a local driver or guide who is knowledgeable about the area's roads and weather.

To sum up, you can either fly into Osvaldo Vieira International Airport or travel across the land border with Senegal or Guinea to reach Guinea-Bissau. Taxis, minibus, and shared vehicles are available for use once inside the nation. It's crucial to plan for your mobility needs and to be ready for a variety of road conditions.

A Tour Of Bissau

Overview and Highlights of the City

The busy marketplaces, rich African culture, and ancient sites may all be found in Bissau, the nation's capital. The architecture of the city, with its majestic structures and lovely squares, is a clear testament to its colonial heritage. Begin your trip by going to Bandim Market, one of West Africa's biggest and busiest markets, where you can take in the atmosphere of the community and shop for a variety of things.

- The National Ethnographic Museum showcases traditional antiques, handicrafts, and exhibitions on regional customs and traditions, giving visitors a look into Guinea-Bissau's rich cultural past. Another interesting site worth seeing is the Presidential Palace, which has a distinctive pink façade. It's a good idea to find out if there are any guided tours available because access to some locations could be limited.

Investigate the Bissau neighborhoods to get a feel for the native way of life. Discover the crowded alleyways of Bandim where you can find lively food vendors and boutiques. Take a break at Praia de Bissau, the city's principal beach, or go on a boat tour of the Geba River to see the surrounding mangroves' natural beauty.

a. Options for Accommodation

A variety of lodging choices are available in Bissau to accommodate diverse spending limits and tastes. For any type of traveler, there are accommodations available, from five-star hotels to guesthouses and affordable alternatives.

Hotels in Guinea-Bissau that range in price from low to high

Low-cost lodging

Joao XXIII Hotel

Djoliba Hotel, Bissau

Inn at Avenue

Inn Central

Bairro Militar Hotel

Romba Hotel

Azalai Hotel - Esquina

Tarrafal Inn

Inn at Bissau

Bula Bula Hotel

High-priced lodgings:

Hotel Ledger Plaza in Bissau

Lisboa Hotel Bissau

The Hotel Ceiba

Azalai Hotel - 24 September

Inn at Imperial

Kalliste Hotel, Bissau

Inn in Miraflores

Inn at Malaika

Ponta Anchaca Hotel

Unity Palace at Hotel Azalai

You can find elegant hotels with cozy rooms, cutting-edge amenities, and frequently a pool and restaurant in the city center. Business people and vacationers looking for a better standard of luxury and service are catered to by these hotels.

- Smaller hotels and guesthouses offer a more personal and regional experience. These inns frequently have a homey environment and provide individualized service. Additionally, some guesthouses could provide chances for cultural immersion and community engagement.

Budget hotels and hostels are available in Bissau for those on a tight budget. These choices offer the bare necessities and are appropriate for those who want to cut expenditures on lodging without sacrificing a pleasurable stay.

b. Food and Dining

There are many different places to eat in Bissau, from regional dishes to foreign delicacies. Tropical fruits, rice, and fish are common ingredients in traditional Bissau-Guinean cuisine. Jollof rice, a savory and spicy rice meal generally served with fish or chicken, is a well-known regional specialty. Fish prepared on the grill or in the oven is another popular and delectable option.

- If you visit Bissau, you should eat some of the regional specialties, like bolinhos de bacalhau (codfish fritters), caldo de peixe (fish stew), and pastéis de milho (corn pastries). These street foods are popular among both locals and tourists since they give you a sense of the regional cuisine.

Restaurants serving Portuguese, Lebanese, and French cuisines, as well as indigenous Bissau-Guinean food, are available in Bissau. For individuals who want to sample a variety of flavors, these alternatives offer a unique dining experience.

c. **Souvenirs and Shopping**

Shopping options in Bissau range from crowded markets to handcrafted goods. For anyone looking for a lively and genuine shopping experience, Bandim Market is a must-stop. Fresh food, spices, fabrics, and handicrafts are just a few of the products you may buy here. When shopping at the market, be prepared to wrangle and bargain over prices.

- Visit Bissau's handcrafted craft marketplaces for one-of-a-kind mementos. A variety of regionally produced products are available at these markets, including wood carvings, pottery, linens, and woven baskets. These handcrafted goods make wonderful unique gifts and keepsakes.

Cities And Regions To Visit

a. Bolama

A UNESCO Biosphere Reserve known as the Bijagós Islands is home to the archipelago known as Bolama. It has a significant architectural history and served as Portuguese Guinea's capital until 1941. Discover the structures from the colonial era, such as the Governor's Palace and the Church of Our Lady of Nazareth. Bolama is the ideal location for leisure and exploration due to its serene beaches and the untouched natural beauty of the nearby islands.

b.Cacheu

- On the Cacheu River stands the historic city of Cacheu. During the colonial era, it was a prominent Portuguese trading post and participated in the slave trade. Visit the

Cacheu Fort, a fortification that has been restored and provides sweeping views of the river and the neighborhood. A museum showcasing local history and culture is also located in the city. Take a stroll along the riverfront promenade while dining at riverbank establishments on regional fare.

- c. **Gabu**: The eastern Guinea-Bissau town of Gabu is well-known for its extensive cultural legacy. It originally served as the seat of the mighty pre-colonial Kingdom of Gabu. Visit the palace of the traditional ruler, where you may learn about the history and customs of the area, and explore the ruins of old stone walls. Gabu also offers an opportunity to experience the regional cultural scene through its lively traditional music and dancing.

d. **Bafata**

The town of Bafata, which is in the center of Guinea-Bissau, is well-known for its bustling marketplaces and historic buildings. Discover the vibrant Bafata Market, where traders provide a wide range of products, such as fresh vegetables, clothing, and crafts. The Governor's Palace and the Cathedral of Bafata are two of the town's many historic structures. Participate in the customary rites and festivals that are frequently held in Bafata to fully experience the culture of the area.

d. **Other Important Locations**

In addition to the cities mentioned above, Guinea-Bissau also has many additional noteworthy locations. Discover the breathtaking scenery of the Bijagós Archipelago, a collection of islands renowned for its immaculate beaches, mangroves, and abundant wildlife. Within the archipelago is the Orango Islands National Park, a protected area providing chances for ecotourism and animal viewing.

- Quinhamel is well renowned for its thriving artistic community, especially for its woodcarving studios. Visit the workshops to see the skill and imagination of regional craftspeople. The area also features stunning beaches that are perfect for unwinding and tanning.

The Cantanhez Forest is a must-see location for anyone who enjoys the outdoors. Many different animals are living in this deep forest, such as monkeys, birds, and reptiles. Take a walk through the forest and see the beauty of the surroundings.

There are countless additional cities, towns, and natural features in Guinea-Bissau that are worth seeing because the nation has a diversified terrain and a rich cultural past. These locations provide one-of-a-kind encounters and chances to fully appreciate Guinea-Bissau's natural splendor and cultural diversity.

Natural Attractions

a. Archipelago of Bijagos

Off the coast of Guinea-Bissau in the Atlantic Ocean is the Bijagós Archipelago, a collection of islands. The magnificent natural beauty, immaculate beaches, and abundant species of this UNESCO Biosphere Reserve are well-known. The principal islands of Bubaque, Bolama, Orango, and Caravela are among the archipelago's 88 or so islands. In addition to spotting a broad range of bird species, marine life, and reptiles, tourists may explore the different ecosystems, which include mangroves, savannahs, and woodlands. Opportunities for ecotourism, birdwatching, boat trips, and cultural exchanges with the nearby Bijagós people can all be found in the Bijagós Archipelago.

b.National Park of the Orango Islands

- The Orango Islands National Park is a protected region recognized for its outstanding biodiversity and is located inside the Bijagós Archipelago. The largest island in the archipelago, Orango Island, is one of the islands included in the park. Numerous animals, including rare and imperiled species like saltwater hippos and sea turtles, can be found in the park. Mangrove forests may be explored, wildlife can be seen, and visitors can learn about local conservation efforts by joining guided excursions. Additionally, the park provides chances for fishing, birdwatching, and interactions with regional cultures.

c. **Cantanhez Forest**

The southern region of Guinea-Bissau is home to the dense tropical forest known as the Cantanhez Forest. This protected area is well known for its abundant biodiversity and acts as a haven for a variety of plant and animal species. Numerous animal species, including monkeys, chimpanzees, duikers, and several bird species, can be found in the forest. Visitors can explore the forest's pathways, spot wildlife, and learn about the diverse ecosystems that coexist there through guided tours and nature hikes, which are offered.

d. **Rio Cacheu Mangroves**

- Along the Cacheu River and its tributaries, there is a sizable mangrove ecosystem known as the Rio Cacheu Mangroves. This marvel of nature is a critical habitat for migratory birds and a significant breeding site for many marine species. To explore the narrow canals, see the distinctive mangrove vegetation, and identify a wide variety of bird species, tourists can go on boat tours or kayak trips.

The mangroves also support a wide variety of fish species, crabs, and other aquatic life, offering an interesting look into Guinea-Bissau's coastal ecosystems.

Additional Natural Wonders

Guinea-Bissau also has more natural beauties worth experiencing in addition to the above-mentioned sites. Beautiful beaches like Praia de Bissau, which provide chances for swimming, tanning, and beachfront relaxation, can be found all over the nation's coastline. The rivers in the nation, such as the Geba and Corubal Rivers, offer beautiful scenery and the opportunity for boat tours for wildlife observation.

- Numerous species of wildlife can be found in the country's different landscapes, which include savannahs, marshes, and estuaries. For the chance to see creatures like antelope, monkeys, crocodiles, and other bird species, nature lovers can go on guided safaris or strolls through the forest.

The natural wonders of Guinea-Bissau provide a singular and untouched experience for tourists looking to discover the nation's biodiversity and natural splendor. These locations highlight the nation's extraordinary natural legacy, whether it is the Bijagós Archipelago, the Orango Islands

National Park, the Cantanhez Forest, the Rio Cacheu Mangroves, or other natural treasures.

Cultural Experience

a.Customary Holidays and Events

Guinea-Bissau is a multiethnic nation with a rich history of customary celebrations and festivities. The lively cultural traditions of the local villages are on display and can be experienced during these celebrations.

- The Tabanka Festival, which takes place in May in Bissau, is one of the most important celebrations. Traditional dance, music, and ceremonies are all featured in this celebration of Balanta culture. Other significant celebrations are the Maio Festival in Bubaque, which highlights Bijagós customs, and the Kussundé Festival in Cacheu, which honors Mandinga culture. Visitors can get a taste of Guinea-Bissau's vibrant costumes, lively music, and authentic cultural expressions by taking part in these festivities.

b. Indigenous Communities and Cultures

There are many indigenous communities in Guinea-Bissau, and each has its unique traditions, rituals, and way of life. Discovering more about these communities' rich cultural legacy is made possible by visiting them. The inhabitants of the Bijagós Archipelago, known as the Bijagós, have a strong bond with both the land and the sea. They continue to engage in their customary agricultural and fishing methods, as well as their spiritual activities and rituals. One of Guinea-Bissau's main ethnic groups, the Balanta, is renowned for its energetic dance displays and agricultural methods. Getting involved with these indigenous tribes reveals details about their way of life, customary crafts, and cultural customs.

c. Historical Sites and Museums

- A glimpse into Guinea-Bissau's remarkable history and cultural heritage can be had at any number of museums and historic locations throughout the nation. The National Ethnographic Museum in Bissau displays a variety of antique items, handicrafts, and exhibitions on regional cultures and traditions. In addition to paying homage to the nation's liberation hero, the Amilcar Cabral Museum offers insights into the struggle for independence.

The Cacheu Fort, a fortress that was important in the slave trade, is located in the historic city of Cacheu. These historical landmarks and museums provide a fuller insight into Guinea-Bissau's past and cultural makeup.

d. Dance and music

- Guinea-Bissau's culture is heavily influenced by music and dance. The nation has a thriving music industry that combines native rhythms with Portuguese, Latin American, and West African influences. In performances, traditional musical instruments like the kora (a string instrument) and the djembe (a drum) are frequently employed. The vibrant and diverse culture of Guinea-Bissau is reflected in the energizing dances and enchanting music. To learn the customary steps and moves, visitors can take part in dancing courses or see live performances in Bissau or other cities.

Visitors can fully immerse themselves in Guinea-Bissau's rich cultural legacy by engaging in cultural activities including attending traditional festivals, meeting with indigenous populations, touring museums and historical sites, and witnessing music and dance performances. The traditions, practices, and aesthetic representations of the nation can be better-understood thanks to these experiences.

Outdoor Activities

a.Wildlife and bird watching

The nation of Guinea-Bissau is a haven for avian aficionados. Numerous bird species are drawn to the nation's diverse environments, which include mangroves, woodlands, wetlands, and coastal regions. Particularly the Bijagós Archipelago is a good location for birding as it is home to numerous resident and migratory birds. Animals including herons, egrets, pelicans, flamingos, and numerous raptors can be seen by visitors. For observing wildlife and birds, the Cantanhez Forest and the Rio Cacheu Mangroves both rank well. It is possible to visit these natural ecosystems and see the magnificent birdlife and other species on guided tours and boat excursions.

b. Trekking and Hiking,

- Trekking and hiking enthusiasts can experience the country of Guinea-Bissau's natural landscapes. With its rich vegetation and trails, the Cantanhez Forest offers a distinctive location for trekking excursions. Visitors can learn about the forest's unique flora and fauna, including monkeys, reptiles, and healing plants, on guided treks. The coastal areas also provide beautiful hikes along cliffs and beaches where you may take in breathtaking ocean views. Employing local guides who are familiar with the area and can offer perceptions of the local environment is advised.

c.Beaches and Water Activities

Guinea-Bissau has a long coastline and a lot of chances for beach and aquatic activities. The unspoiled beaches, like Praia de Bissau, provide the best surroundings for swimming, tanning, and beachcombing. To discover the vibrant marine life and coral reefs, you can snorkel or dive in the pristine waters of the Bijagós Archipelago. The calm waters of rivers and estuaries are ideal for paddleboarding and kayaking. Some beachfront hotels additionally provide facilities for renting out equipment and participating in water sports.

d.Fishing and Boating

- Fishing enthusiasts will find paradise in Guinea-Bissau. Tarpon, barracuda, and snapper are just a few of the many fish species that inhabit the nation's rivers, mangroves, and coastal regions. It is possible to schedule fishing excursions with regional guides or fishing charters, giving one the chance to try out traditional fishing techniques or sport fishing. Another well-liked pastime in Guinea-Bissau is boating, which enables tourists to travel the coastline, navigate the rivers, and discover the

Bijagós Archipelago. It is possible to schedule boat cruises to explore uninhabited islands, see wildlife, and take in the picturesque grandeur of the nearby waterways.

Whether it's birdwatching and wildlife viewing, climbing and trekking, participating in water sports along the coast, or taking fishing and boating excursions, these outdoor activities provide an opportunity to get in touch with Guinea-Bissau's natural environment. The nation's varied topography and abundant biodiversity offer a variety of opportunities for outdoor enthusiasts to explore and take part in their favorite activities.

Practical Travel Advice

a.Regional Customs and Protocol

In Guinea-Bissau, it is highly important to show respect towards elders. Elderly persons should always be greeted first and treated with respect.

- Important cultural characteristics include politeness and friendliness. Give individuals a firm handshake and behave politely and respectfully at all times.

  When visiting rural areas or places of worship, dress modestly. For ladies in particular, it is advisable to cover your shoulders and knees.

Before shooting pictures of individuals, get their consent, especially in distant areas or during cultural events.

Before entering a person's home or a place of worship, it is traditional to take off your shoes.

b Transportation Safety Advice

There aren't many public transit choices in Guinea-Bissau. In cities and towns, mini buses and shared taxis, also referred to as "toca-tocas," are the most widely used modes of transportation.

- Consider using trustworthy cab services and use caution when using public transit, especially at night.

The state of the roads might be difficult, particularly outside of big cities. Drive carefully and pay attention to livestock, cyclists, and pedestrians on the roads.

Make sure you have valid international driving licenses if you intend to rent a car and educate yourself with local traffic laws.

When visiting isolated locations or taking longer excursions, it is advised to use local drivers or guides.

c.Suggested Tour Companies and Guides

You can improve your vacation experience in Guinea-Bissau by using local tour companies and guides. They can guarantee safety, offer insightful information, and promote cross-cultural communication.

Choose reliable tour companies that have local knowledge by doing your research. Look for recommendations and examine traveler evaluations. Look for tour leaders who are educated about the area's natural wonders, culture, and history. With their knowledge, they may deepen your understanding of the places you visit and enhance your journey.

d.Important Items to Pack

Guinea-Bissau has a tropical environment, thus it is advised to wear light, breathable clothing. Bring clothing that will shield you from the sun and insect stings.

It's imperative to wear comfortable walking shoes or sandals, especially if you intend to see natural landmarks or participate in outdoor activities.

- Don't forget to bring sunscreen, bug repellant, and a hat for sun protection.
  Given that Guinea-Bissau uses various voltage standards and electrical outlets, a universal power adapter is helpful.

Carrying a modest first aid bag containing common drugs, bandages, and any necessary prescription prescriptions is advised.

Think about bringing a reusable water bottle on your trip to reduce plastic waste and keep you hydrated.

These useful hints can make for an easier and more pleasurable trip to Guinea-Bissau. You may make the most of your trip in this dynamic West African nation by adhering to local customs, remaining safe while traveling, using reliable tour operators or guides, and packing the necessities.

Language and Useful Phrase

Foundational Expressions and Phrases

Welcome: Olá

Salutations: Bom dia

Salutations: Boa tarde

Hello and good night.

Obrigado (for men)/Obrigada (for women) means "thank you."

Sure: Sim

No: Não

Please: Please

I'm sorry. Com licença

Sorry: Apologies

What's up?: How are you?

I'm unable to understand:

Can you assist me? Can you help me?

Where is that? Where is it...?

What is the price? What does it cost?

Eu gostaria de...: I desire...

Overview of Local Language

Portuguese is the official language of Guinea-Bissau. Nevertheless, several regional tongues are spoken all around the nation, reflecting its numerous ethnic groups. Among the well-known regional tongues are:

- **Crioulo**: A sizable section of the population speaks this Creole language. It combines African languages, Portuguese, and other elements. Portuguese continues to be the preferred language for official communication, even though many locals, particularly in urban areas, can comprehend and speak Crioulo.

Mandinka: One of the largest ethnic groups in Guinea-Bissau, the Mandinka speak a widely used language. When communicating with the nearby Mandinka people, learning a few simple Mandinka words and phrases can be helpful.

- Balanta, Fula, and other regional tongues are spoken in Guinea-Bissau, which is home to numerous ethnic groups. Other languages spoken by their respective populations are Balanta and Fula. Even while it might not be realistic to learn every local language, people will enjoy it if you show an interest in and respect for the variety of languages.

Although English is not frequently spoken in Guinea-Bissau, you can run into some locals with rudimentary English language abilities, especially in tourist hotspots or major cities. To help you communicate when traveling in Guinea-Bissau, it is advised that you acquire a few fundamental Portuguese words and phrases or that you keep a language dictionary or translation app close at hand.

Safety And Health

Travelers' health and safety in Guinea-Bissau:

a.Immunizations and medical preparation

- To get the most recent information on advised vaccines, it is advised to speak with a healthcare professional or travel medicine specialist before flying to Guinea-Bissau. Hepatitis A and B, typhoid, yellow fever, and tetanus shots are frequently recommended for visitors visiting Guinea-Bissau.

It is crucial to take antimalarial medication as directed by your doctor because malaria is common in Guinea-Bissau. Additionally, taking precautions against mosquito bites, such as applying insect repellent and donning long sleeves, might lessen the chance of contracting diseases carried by mosquitoes.

A basic travel medical kit with necessary prescriptions, such as pain relievers, antidiarrheal drugs, and sticky bandages, is advised. Make sure you have plenty of prescription pills you need in your bag.

b. Travel protection

It is strongly advised to purchase comprehensive travel insurance before visiting Guinea-Bissau. This should cover personal property, travel cancellation or interruption, medical costs, and emergency medical evacuation.

Carefully read the insurance policy to comprehend the coverage, exclusions, and steps involved in filing a claim. While traveling, keep a copy of your insurance policy and emergency phone numbers with you.

c. Emergency Phone Numbers

- During your visit to Guinea-Bissau, it's crucial to have access to emergency contact information. Save the phone numbers for the police, fire department, and other local emergency services in your phone, or keep them written down somewhere that is convenient to you.

Keep the contact details of the hotel or tour operator you are using close to hand in case you want assistance or experience an emergency.

11.4 Awareness of Crime and Scams

While traveling in Guinea-Bissau is generally regarded as safe, it is still important to use caution and pay attention to your surroundings. Don't flaunt expensive stuff or carry a lot of cash around with you.

- Be on the lookout for pickpockets and small-time theft in crowded places like marketplaces or public transportation. Use bags with anti-theft measures and keep your possessions locked up.

- Keep up with any travel warnings or advisories issued by the embassy or consulate of your country.

Be wary of potential tourist scams like inflated prices for services or goods, unlicensed tour guides, or phony police officers. Be cautious of deals that appear too good to be true and only use reputed tour guides and travel providers.

While traveling in Guinea-Bissau, it's critical to put your health and safety first. You can contribute to ensuring a safe and secure journey by taking the required health precautions, having the appropriate travel insurance, knowing who to contact in case of emergency, and remaining watchful against potential crime and scams.

Sustainable Travel and Responsible Tourism

Create information on responsible tourism and sustainable travel.

12.1 Environmental and Cultural Considerations

12.2 Encourage regional initiatives

12.3 Leaving No Trace and Reducing Impact

a. Environmental and Cultural Considerations

- Be respectful of regional traditions, customs, and cultural practices. Spend some time getting to know the locals and treat them with respect as you interact with them. Dress modestly, obtain consent before photographing others, and observe any rules or regulations at religious or cultural institutions.

Be environmentally conscious and behave responsibly. Avoid leaving behind trash, and dispose of it appropriately. Conserve water and energy, especially if there may be a shortage of these resources. By staying on approved pathways and refraining from any activity that can damage the environment, you can show respect for protected areas and the habitats of wildlife.

b. **Encourage regional initiatives**

- Select lodgings, travel companies, and restaurants that place a strong emphasis on sustainability and community support. Look for eco-friendly lodgings that apply policies like trash minimization, energy saving, and encouragement of nearby employment and enterprises.

Look for locally owned and run establishments, such as tour operators, artisanal shops, and dining establishments. This promotes a more equitable distribution of the economic benefits of tourism throughout the local community.

- Participate in cultural encounters and pursuits that directly profit neighborhood communities. This could be taking part in customary activities and festivals, visiting community-based tourism initiatives, or helping out local artists by purchasing their goods.

c. Leaving No Trace and Reducing Impact

Reduce your environmental effect to engage in responsible travel. Use eco-friendly toiletries, carry a reusable water bottle, and steer clear of single-use plastics wherever you can. Respect wildlife by keeping a safe distance from animals and refraining from interfering with their natural activity.

- Follow the "Leave No Trace" guidelines when visiting natural places, such as parks and reserves: pack out all trash, stick to authorized routes, and avoid destroying vegetation or wildlife habitats. Avoid taking natural or cultural relics home as mementos because doing so can harm the ecosystem and the community's history.

Take your travels' carbon footprint into account. When possible, choose sustainable transportation methods like taking public transit or using shared vehicle services. Support credible carbon offset programs that make investments in renewable energy or environmental conservation to offset your carbon emissions.

You may support the residents, encourage a good impact on the area, and contribute to the preservation of Guinea-Bissau's cultural heritage and natural environment by engaging in responsible tourism and sustainable travel.

Travel kit for traveling to Guinea-Bissau:

essential records

Passport

Visa, if necessary

Information on travel insurance

First Aid and Health:

prescribed drugs (together with a copy of the prescription)

Basic first-aid supplies, including bandages, antiseptic wipes, and painkillers

DEET-containing insect repellent

Use sunblock with a high SPF.

salts for oral rehydration

tablets or filters for water purification

Accessories and Clothes

Clothing that is light and airy and is appropriate for
a tropical climate

comfortable sandals or walking shoes

Sun protection hat

Swimwear

In case of rain, use a raincoat or poncho.

(For covering shoulders or going to sacred sites) a
sarong or thin scarf

Miscellaneous and Electronics:

a worldwide power adapter

portable power bank charger

Shampoo, toothpaste, toothbrushes, and other amenities in travel-size

(Compact and quick-drying) travel towel

(To secure your possessions) A travel lock

Wallet or money belt for travel

portable laundry detergent for washing clothes by hand

Grass-fed snacks with a reusable water bottle

Having fun and communicating:

books about travel or offline maps

dictionaries or translation software

Pen and travel journal

alternatives for entertainment (music, literature, e-books, etc.)

Mobile phones and e-readers are examples of portable electronic devices.

Keep in mind to pack lightly and take the weight limitations of your preferred mode of transportation into account. Checking the local laws and customs surrounding attire and any products that might be restricted in Guinea-Bissau is also a good idea.

The essentials for your trip to Guinea-Bissau should be included in this travel kit, keeping you organized, cozy, and ready to make the most of your travel experience. Depending on your preferences and requirements, adjust it as necessary.

Packing list for Guinea-Bissau:

Medications on prescription:

Bring enough of your prescription drugs with you to last the entire trip. Carrying copies of the prescriptions and any other necessary medical records is also advisable in case they are required for customs or medical reasons.

Standard First Aid Kit

For covering small cuts, scrapes, or blisters, use adhesive bandages and sterile dressings.

Before applying bandages or dressings, clean the wound with antiseptic wipes or a solution.

Include over-the-counter painkillers for headaches, muscular aches, and other minor discomfort, such as acetaminophen or ibuprofen.

Antihistamines: These medicines can help treat allergic responses and symptoms brought on by bug bites or stings.

Tweezers and scissors are useful tools for bandaging wounds or splinter removal.

Bandages or dressings can be fastened in place using adhesive tape and safety pins.

For more serious wounds or injuries that call for more extensive bandaging or compression, gauze pads, and elastic bandages are helpful.

- Disposable gloves: To prevent yourself and others from contracting dangerous illnesses when delivering first aid, it's crucial to have gloves on hand.
  A portable, digital thermometer helps keep an eye on body temperature in the event of illness.
- any particular medicines or equipment that you need to treat your allergies or medical issues.

Bug repellent (including DEET):

Given that Guinea-Bissau is in a tropical area, it's crucial to avoid getting bitten by insects. Because DEET is effective against mosquitoes, which can spread diseases like malaria and dengue fever, go with an insect repellent that contains it. When reapplying, follow the directions on the product.

High SPF sun protection:

- A high sun protection factor (SPF) sunscreen is essential for the tropical climate to shield your skin from damaging UV rays. Choose a broad-spectrum sunscreen that delivers both UVA and UVB ray protection. It should be liberally applied to all exposed skin, and it should be reapplied frequently, especially after swimming or perspiring.

Salts for oral rehydration

It's crucial to drink plenty of water in hot weather and when exercising. Electrolytes lost through sweating are replaced by oral rehydration salts, which are especially helpful in cases of diarrhea or vomiting. For proper usage, adhere to the directions on the packaging.

Tablets or a filter for water filtration:

In Guinea-Bissau, it is advised to consume filtered water to prevent contracting waterborne diseases. To ensure that the water you drink is safe, carry water purification pills or a portable water filter. Use tablets or filters according to the directions supplied to properly cleanse water before drinking.

During your travels in Guinea-Bissau, these health and first aid supplies will assist you in taking care of minor wounds, shielding yourself from insects and sunburn, and keeping hydrated. It's always a good idea to speak with a medical expert before your trip to get specialized medical advice and make sure you have all the meds and supplies you'll need for your unique requirements.

Printed in Great Britain
by Amazon

46778644R00050